A PACKET OF POEMS
FOR EZRA POUND

The Ezra Pound Center for Literature
at the University of New Orleans

The Ezra Pound Center for Literature Book Series is a project dedicated to publishing a variety of scholarly and literary works relevant to Ezra Pound and Modernism, including new critical monographs on Pound and/or other Modernists, scholarly studies related to Pound and his legacy, edited collections of essays, volumes of original poetry, reissued books of importance to Pound scholarship, translations, and other works.

Series Editor: John Gery, University of New Orleans

Editorial Advisory Board

Barry Ahearn, Tulane University
Massimo Bacigalupo, University of Genoa
A. David Moody (Emeritus), University of York
Ira B. Nadel, University of British Columbia
Marjorie Perloff, University of Southern California
Tim Redman, University of Texas at Dallas
Richard Sieburth, New York University
Demetres P. Tryphonopoulos, Brandon University
Emily Mitchell Wallace, Bryn Mawr College

Also Available in the Ezra Pound Center for Literature Book Series

William Pratt, Editor, *The Imagist Poem: Modern Poetry in Miniature*
Patrizia de Rachewiltz, *Trespassing*
Caterina Ricciardi, John Gery, and Massimo Bacigalupo, Editors, *I poeti della Sala Capizucchi/The Poets of the Sala Capizucchi*
Zhaoming Qian, Editor, *Modernism and the Orient*
John Gery, Daniel Kempton, and H. R. Stoneback, Editors, *Imagism: Essays on Its Initiation, Impact and Influence*
Catherine E. Paul, *Fascist Directive: Ezra Pound and Italian Cultural Nationalism*

A PACKET OF POEMS
FOR EZRA POUND

POETRY FROM THE EZRA POUND
INTERNATIONAL CONFERENCE JULY 2015

EDITED BY CATHERINE PAUL &
JUSTIN KISHBAUGH

CLEMSON
UNIVERSITY
PRESS

CONTENTS

Editors' Introduction

A *Packet of Poems for Ezra Pound* brings us back, as nearly as possible in book form, to the poetry reading that took place in Dorf Tirol, Italy on July 8, 2015 at 8 p.m., as a part of that summer's Ezra Pound International Conference. The poetry reading is a crucial part of every biannual EPIC, a reminder that Pound's poetry is no corpse to be studied only as a part of the past, but rather a constant instigator of creative work, an inspiration for living poets.

After a summer rain that brought a moment of cool to an exceptionally hot week in Dorf Tirol and pushed the reading indoors, the sun returned that evening, dousing the big open window behind the poets with waning evening light. Arranged in an arc that allowed us to see them all together even as each read individually, the stage contained an array of rich talent that this anthology aims to reunite in book form, a memento of an evening well spent.

We title this collection *A Packet of Poems for Ezra Pound* because that evening's poetry reading was preceded by a reading from W. B. Yeats's collection *A Packet for Ezra Pound*. Published first on its own in 1929, *A Packet* became the preface to a second edition of *A Vision* in 1937. As we know, Ezra and Dorothy Pound settled in Rapallo in 1924. Their presence helped the town appeal to Yeats, who moved there with his wife, George, in February 1928, searching for the rest, sun, and warmth necessary to help him recuperate from illness. Almost immediately, Yeats began imagining an essay about Rapallo as a new introduction to *A Vision*. This fascinating and esoteric work originated in communication with spirits, and it outlines a system to explain human personality, creativity, and history, as well as cycles of life and death. The balcony of the Pounds' top-floor apartment, with its view to the Golfo di Tigullio, became the setting for numerous conversations between the poets—and subject matter for *A Packet*. As Yeats wrote to Lady Gregory shortly after his arrival, "This is an indescribably lovely place—some little Greek town one imagines—there is a passage in Keats describing just such a town. Here I shall put off the bitterness of Irish quarrels, and write my most amiable verses. They are already, though I dare not write, crowding my head."

Pound connected Yeats with other artists in Rapallo, and Yeats and Pound discussed poetry, politics, translating Guido Cavalcanti, the ethnographic writings of Leo Frobenius, modern music, and Wyndham Lewis's theories of modernism. Within the first month, Yeats began to envisage a new book about his literary community there. The centerpiece was to be Cavalcanti's *canzone* "Donna mi prega." As Yeats explained in early March 1928: "I am now working again (though only on alternate days) & what I am doing is a comment on a philosophical poem of Guido Cavalcanti's, translated by Ezra Pound. . . . I think of calling the book 'Siris'; it is about Rapallo, Ezra & the literary movements of our time all deduced from Guido's poem, as Berkeley in his 'Siris' deduced all from tar-water."

This essay became "Rapallo," and in early drafts Yeats discusses *The Cantos* at greater length than in the published text, in one passage concluding that "the effect is that of some complicated ever changing vision seen under our closed eyelids as we are dropping off to sleep."

Almost immediately, Yeats connected this new piece to *A Vision*, and by November 1928 he was calling the book "either 'A Packet' or 'A Packet for Ezra Pound.'" Yeats describes the contents: "It contains first a covering letter to Ezra saying that I offer him the contents, urging him not to be elected to the Senate of his country and telling him why. Then comes a long essay already finished, the introduction to the new edition of *A Vision* and telling all about its origin, and then I shall wind up with a description of Ezra feeding the cats ('some of them are so ungrateful,' T. S. Eliot says), of Rapallo and Ezra's poetry—some of which I greatly admire, indeed *Personae* is a great excitement to me."

A Packet for Ezra Pound was first published as a stand-alone volume in 1929 by Yeats's sisters' Cuala Press. In a section of "Rapallo"

POETRY FROM EPIC 2015   ix

published in the Cuala version but not in *A Vision*, Yeats writes:
"Four weeks ago I read poetry again after four years philosophical
study; at first it was faint like an old faded letter, and then an excite-
ment that I had not felt for years. I read [. . .] Ezra Pound's 'Personæ.'
One is a harder judge of a friend's work than of a stranger's because
one knows his powers so well that his faults seem perversity, or we
do not know his powers and think he should go our way and not
his, and then all in a moment we see his work as a whole and judge
as with the eyes of a stranger. [. . .] I had never understood . . .
that the translations from Chinese, from Latin, from Provencal, are
as much a part of his original work, as much chosen as to theme,
as much characterised as to style, as the vituperation, the railing,
which I had hated but which now seem a necessary balance." In
1937, *A Packet* became a kind of preface for *A Vision*, albeit with a
change in the order of the contents.

On the evening of our readings in Dorf Tirol, we did not read
Yeats's "Introduction to *A Vision*," but only "Rapallo" and "To Ezra
Pound," the first and last essays. "Rapallo" opens with a description
of that town and its appeal, appropriately read by Rapallo-native
Massimo Bacigalupo. Alec Marsh took us into Yeats's ruminations
on Pound's politics, and Bernard Dew delivered Yeats's rather-con-
fusing-in-itself attempt to make sense of the structure of the *Cantos*.
Peter Liebregts, whose scholarship encompasses both poets, read
Yeats's brief attempt to connect his own thinking and writing to
Pound's work. Roxana Preda read a delightful passage of the essay
that remembers Pound's conversations with cats, and Ron Smith
delivered Yeats's concern about Pound's and Maud Gonne's shared
combativeness. Justin Kishbaugh read Yeats's wondering about his
own religion and how it differs from his experience in churches, be-
fore Catherine Paul read the closing of Yeats's essay, with its sense of
relief that the work of *A Vision* is finished, leaving him free to relish
the pleasures of Rapallo.

Yeats opens "To Ezra Pound" with an injunction almost cruel,
given Pound's political ambitions: "Do not be elected to the Senate
of your country." David Cappella opened the reading of this essay,
and Walter Baumann added Yeats's warning that politics do not suit

poets. Anderson Araujo and Andy Trevathan shared the reading of a paragraph written for Pound in which Yeats tries to condense a summary of his own historical and mythic thinking. Catherine Paul offered Yeats's acknowledgment that *A Vision* might be just the kind of book that Pound would hate, before John Gery closed the reading with Yeats's full quotation of Pound's poem, "The Return."

These essays and their backstory reveal a conversation between two poets crucial to both their work. The Rapallo chapter is but one in their long and important, if also vexed, literary and personal relationship. Without this connection—which was sometimes collaboration, sometimes influence, sometimes almost combat—both poets' work would have been vastly different, so our reading of these essays was a celebration of their poetic relationship.

The poetry reading that night similarly celebrated conversation among poets. The readers at EPIC are frequently described as "Poundian poets": poets who in some way see a connection between their work and Pound's. And as the poems in this anthology demonstrate, that connection is a rich and multilingual one indeed. We have included as many of the poets from that reading as possible, and we print the contributions by the poets in the order in which they read. In some cases, the contents here differ from what was read in Dorf Tirol, but in all cases, the works included are "Poundian poems." We hope this book will transport you to—or enable you to experience for the first time—that suddenly sunny July evening in Dorf Tirol.

All quotations from Yeats's drafts and from *A Packet for Ezra Pound* are taken from W. B. Yeats, *A Vision: The Revised 1937 Edition*, Collected Works 14, ed. Margaret Mills Harper and Catherine E. Paul (New York: Scribner, 2015).

DAVID CAPPELLA

DEAD POETS TRIPTYCH

(for Ron Smith)

Cimitero inglese di Roma

The ephemeral hugs it,
the Aurelian Wall. Shade
from the cypress looms over
the graveyard. A moldy hush
spreads through me, a verdigris
like the black lichen that gnaws
edges of the marble headstones.

I

Against my better judgment,
because who cannot favor
the virginal words, exquisite
and beautiful, of the boy
poet who knew death, slowly,
spit blood for the sublime,
I sit across from his grave.

I note the sun, wispy clouds,
the fitting gentle breeze,
the purple irises spiking
beside the simple gravestone,
those deathless, mocking words
that bring the eyes back to earth.
Newly planted sod greens the site.

Above, on the half round top
a crudely carved lyre covers

half the stone. I stare at it.
Its body space is odd, filled
with only four strings subtly
fanning to the left, the right
is empty, missing three strings

in what has to be, for me,
a seven-stringed instrument.
Everyone knows the symbol
of this four-stringed lyre. It can
be played that way. Sitting here,
pondering words and life,
I want the seven-stringed lyre
to be on this marble slab,
its range—its treble, its base
extended for a full sound.
Three extra strings etched from yoke
to the bridge could strike a chord
to chase this clinging hush. I
cannot grieve for this dead poet

or for any. Life was his grief.
My friend says poets break their hearts
over it. That is a Truth;
and Beauty is the being
here, an old man, pretending
to make a crude lyre chiseled
on a headstone what it's not.

II

I imagined climbing a mountain. The stone path
to your grave rose through rows of the dead.
My heart leapt in the slow walk up.
You wanted all travelers to go to Rome.
There I stood, gazing down at the marble slab.
Under it you slumber in your death.

Blanketed in earth, the remote world you dreamt
in words I hope for your sake you dream now.
So young, I sat in class, let my fancy fly out

the window chasing your poems, the way they
seemed to chase the invisible. I yearned
for your philosophy back then. Now,

un vecchio uomo, I want to tell you this
where whatever remains of you lies:
you were right about the universe.

Standing here in the shady stillness
my back aches, a dull throb not unlike
the ache I felt in your words as they strived

to seek the sublime. It's not a bad pursuit
to struggle with words, to use them
like a gold pan to sift for deeper meaning,

to prospect for what you cannot see
but know to be real—those ethereal nuggets
I hope you've discovered in your deadly silence.

I—a living silence—do not brood now.
Instead I welcome this momentary solitude
where I try to capture my own remotest secrets.

III

Oh Nunzio, I had forgotten you were here!
You've announced yourself to me—a graveyard miracle.
Fellow Italian-American, my spontaneous visitor, who belongs
here with the others, you who wanted a home, any home, somewhere.
Yes, drunken angel waif, inebriated American elegist
who yearned to announce miracles to a desperate world.

The last time I saw you, you mumbled, bubbled, blurted
dark, drug-laden phrases to Ginsberg trying to read.
He said, "Please, Gregory, do not interrupt anymore."
The dark currents subsided, you fell back in your seat,
knocked down by yourself again—drowned . . .
drowned in what sea? Yourself?

You worked it all out on your own. Had to. I admired that.
I knew what you meant, *amico mio*, when you said,
"I'd rather have a little bit of knowledge than a whole lot of faith."
No wonder "the quietude of poetry" brought calm
when it provided you, usually in the hour of the wolf—
that deep, dark of night—some solace. It's yours forever now.

Under Shelley's shadow, the simple marble square
rests succinct, elegant. The single word under your name—*poeta*—
heralds your spirit. The green shrubbery that squares all
but the slab's base—a wreath-like halo for you, poet urchin
who knew various hells including the one that was your life.
I imagine you singing a lilting melody like Blake when he sang
on his death bed. Maybe in a heaven, maybe in a hell,
did you try to sneak a miracle knowing you never could?

What message do you have, as I ponder why your baptized name
is left off the stone? Nunzio, *dimmi caro*, why did you do that?
You, pesky poet archangel, so loved. An anonymous visitor
has left a single red rose, an hour from fresh. Life ripples
through me while I read your epitaph again, stare at the flower.
For a moment, I feel afloat, drifting in your words—
E il naufragar m'è dolce in questo mare.

Schloss Brunnenburg

The vineyard rows like lines
of poetry stretched on a page
traverse green valley hills.

Ripening apples, pears
hang on boughs along
the narrow road down

to the castle. In the distance
a tractor engine cranks
along a hidden road.

Birds chirp in leafy branches.
Their songs echo in the ravine
below Schloss Tirol

where hawks soar.
The mountains: silent,
their jagged peaks fragments—
remote in the mind.

PATRIZIA DE RACHEWILTZ

CANTO

(for my mother)

You are the ring in the tree,
the shadowed brow, the hard resin.
From your filled ancestry seeps the sap
as it grows, filled with the pomegranate, outer love.
Limpid tender root anchored in the lake,
braided hair in your sleep—
in one single bough of time
two boughs. The whim against blinds and beams
has given way to the night of the mountain.
Against you hurled an infrequent rival,
a succession of sunsets, leading to splendor.

The Canto goes on consuming sky,
its vale of tears inherited.
Poets die prisoners
but not the dawn.
Tree trunk Brancusian becomes light
and the bird is looking for you.
Not many flowers I picked but oceans,
to me, as slender plumed swallow,
you gave way to wings and a solid perch.

At last the light diffuses my first wails,
and I listen to the sighing of the wind.
Transparent tree,
our home has radiant thresholds.
I seek beyond time and find
there is peace,
as your voice sings to me old lullabies.

JUSTIN KISHBAUGH

Freedom Fries

If not for the Eiffel Tower
being overrun by giant
black widow spiders,
the war may have never
stopped. The government
had stored enough oat meal
to feed its entire population
for at least six more months,
if not the entire year.
That same day, I found
you in Mr. McGregor's corner
store. You were finishing
your milkshake as I
walked in. You probably
wondered who told me
about your father, and
why I was being so generous,
but that wasn't the time
to discuss details. I tried
to seem unaffected,
but couldn't escape
the lipstick marks
on your straw.

"THE BIG PAYBACK"

By the time we left the soiree, the sky had already begun to fade in a beautiful sorbet of Bob Ross oranges and pinks. Spring seemed to be exploding in all its pastel grandeur and we had dressed fittingly. She wore a wonderful ensemble composed of three-and-a-half shades of complementary pinks that she painstakingly selected from the wares of all the finest boutiques in a three-borough radius. I was dressed in a mint-green Oxford shirt, gray micropolyester trousers, and a golden tie that smartly matched her highlights. We were strolling west, toward the mountains, letting culture's bouquet test our palates when we stumbled into what seemed the makings of high conversation. After a few false starts, which we duly disregarded, I asked her what she believed was the all-time greatest robe. After only a brief moment of thought, she offered the one James Brown throws off when pretending to leave the stage. Impressed with the quality and quickness of her response, I nodded my head in recognition. Seemingly pleased with my reaction and the possibilities of the question posed, she sauntered to a planter just off the sidewalk. Bending over, she placed her nose just above a yellow tulip and somewhat flippantly said, ". . . Or the shroud of Turin." I casually, yet with perfect posture, approached her and replied, "Yes dear, but a shroud, technically, is not a robe." "Technically," she reiterated as she broke the flower's stem and placed it into my chest pocket, "it could be considered a burial robe."

L'Eclisse

When Monica became
a flash in the rain
and danced like an African

Alain Delon wore Dior cologne
to wander the streets of Rome

on a picnic in a field
they gaze in different directions

a tug on too short jean shorts
and an uncomfortable stare
with a little bit of glitter
and perfume in her hair

their cigarettes dangle
while their arms tangle
and he doesn't care

but since they're there
he mentions his career
as a financier and calculates

    several years

later he'll send her a letter
to question whether they're better
together or alone

but she'll find his enquiries a bore
and wish she didn't love him
or loved him much more.

THREE FROM *FOR THE BLUE FLASH*

i

With the panels open
her cat's eyes gaze
while visitors make
offerings for prosperity
she admires his gift
of hairpins wrapped
in an honorable act
he sits before her
bare white frame

ii

He reads to her
of a painter and his muse
who exposed her neck
and offered her eyes
like a cloud finally
loose from its moorings

iii

On a bent birch
weighted with snow
a cardinal stands out more
vibrant in the winter nothing
more vibrant than her eyes

DAVID MOODY

Olga Rudge: To Her Memory

i

She was 90
and I was to "look after her," she
    the lightest of travellers,
and for all of that journey
her conversation gave pleasure
    and instruction
    For nine untiring hours
she drew from the clear well of memory—
    anecdotes about Pound and the *Cantos*,
        and a childhood ride
        out to Mt. Chocorua
        "For the purity of the air,"

It could have been *The Aspern Papers*
with the tables turned—she telling me all
    just as she wanted it told.

ii

A few years on, in her daughter's house,
her mind gone
    far back into memory
and the gracious manners still all there
as of Paris and the *salons*,
not as patina
    but like bone
    or sculpted stone
        bearing an old civilization.

iii

Again some years
and she had been listening to music
in her large, light-filled room,
and her bright gaze was centred
    upon something very far off.

Her courtesy was unfaltering—
And "who *was* that?" she queried
    as I closed the door.

iv Their letters

How constant she was
through all his vicissitudes
    to the god she discerned in E. P.
And that did not mean she thought *him* a god
        she reassured him

Her centre a man whose centre was his genius
Her spirit a match for his

Only after ten years and the child
did she get to him

Her best years a solitary confinement
imposed by his respect for respectability

then cut off by his confinement, and his blackouts
for another fifteen

What is important, they had agreed, is not
what happens, but how one takes it

"J'ayme donc je suis"

Fifty years together and not together
until the last "silent" decade

Secret amour, unacknowledged *compagne*
ménagère à trois, or à quatre with the lion cub

But to end he must come to her house
as to Persephone's bower
and repenting think of her
"among the emparadysed spirits."

From the Chinese

THE DARKENING GARDEN

Sunset, and the clouds thin out,
   the sky fills with colour
      while shadows merge;
A breath of wind stirs
   the dark curtain of trees, green
      where the last light reaches.

The reflected west fades in the window,
   the garden becomes lost in itself;
on the pool a faint pallor glimmers . . .
   Then only the cold sounds of autumn.

Would that my love and I were together
   our two voices making one chord
      then each lost in the other.

—Xie Chuang (421–466)

At the Hermit's Well, Evening

Spring,
    bright moss
        covers
            the stone rim,
    the bucket
        drops
            into darkness . . .
    The old one,
        recluse,
            slowly fills
    drinking in
        the deepening
            shadows.

—Sikong Shu (740–790)

Printed on Snow

A fine line
of small prints
across the snow

(a field-mouse
running?)
stops short

in mid-field—
at its end
a wing-print

on the snow
delicate & precise
shows an owl

stooped there,
so delicate and
so precise.

STEPHEN ROMER

Roman Stele, Ravenna

Frank eyes, appraising eyes,
—they inquire, also—
could he manage men, drive a road through rock
raise an aqueduct
from the sweet springs of Carmel
to water Caesarea,
get up a Circus up—?

The drilled eyeballs
find me out, the dry gaze
—this one's no grafter, and no
committee man, useless to the
distension of Empire, he lacks
our Roman energy,
the steady hands
of the administrator
careful of the coming in
and going out of the fleet . . .

(Caesar I worshipped, the coveted
purple book of boyhood,
his cropped hair, a handsome
senior prefect with a baton,
a caped dictator
on his podium!
—better than parsing
Virgil on lonely evenings
Aeneid Fit V;
I cannot
construe history).

Or that mumbo-jumbo
coming from the East
the man-god shorn
of thunderbolt and sword,
the babe is born!
Unnatural terror
their sloe eyes stare upon
high in the vaults there
a baffling trance
of revelation.

My shrewd provincial governor
entrusts his family
to no such thing
nor to the thunderer
and his rout in heaven
but rather, the Matriarch above
the Spouse by his side
and little Princeps
down below
peeping from the stele
he offers them all
Dis Manibus,

shades of hearth and family
the only ones
worth having in the end,
crowding palely
round the cradle
possibly
even useful, he has
weighed their worth
—a modest hope.

Scrambling after Ruskin

Poring over the Romanesque,
endeavouring to learn good ornament,

Saint Hilaire de Poitiers, Saint Jean de Cole,
the bare lofty cavern of St Amand de Coly

where the Black Prince once rode by
and smashed a hole in the transept wall;

verdigris deposit high on pillars
as if the sea had submerged it and receded,

Ruskin banging on about carving
direct carving of the stone,

while over my head, on my own roof
the old red tiles are shaved and the new slate clipped

and the whole sealed lightly in
with a light cement,

two brothers, two trecento heads
bobbing about my roof

handling the beams and the slats
with care and with grace:

these are the artisans, they feel pride
in their materials, and in the thing well done.

IN A PROVENÇAL GARDEN

*There is some proportion between the fine thing held in the mind, and
the inferior thing ready for instant consumption.*
                                                    —Ezra Pound

To give back simply, as the stones give back
warmth at the end of a day
that seethed and gurgled through Triton's gums

who watched you from below,
your svelte shadow, white form,
snatchable into the depths

where you change in the downward struggle
lion-headed goat-saddled serpent-tailed,
bronze chimera and are his at last; but you surface

and lie down naked on the flags to bronze,
a beauty of body and proportion
pleasing to the Greek, replete.

Where the garden folds down
its terraces to the roughest patch
I like to lurk, a wrinkled creature

of the heat, in the parched land, with thyme,
and the invisible cicada who stops singing.
Let us be cast in bronze forever!

But I find you in meditation, in Mary's colour,
the blue convolvulus, the sensual flower
you no longer see, but look beyond or through,

and the stones cool and the night draws on.

Torcello

Discouraged, cowled, broken-soled,
but brushed by kairos, time's arrow,
you walked on the ice, scarlet gleams

cast by a theology of terror
demeaning to you, Christ the assayer
fueling the fiery crack,

and worms in the sockets
of the naked pallid forked—
a prey to the teeming image, even here!

All of us, then, on the little jetty
of the glacial exarchate,
the damned with the saved

waiting, anxious to be taken off,
and you, yellow-eyed, absorbed
by the *formula virtutis,* was it then

you withdrew into your faith
where I could not follow, a quiet space
floated within the other apse,

Hodigitria, and the child, who will save?

J. R. FORMAN

PAPER MONEY

And it's a good thing too
'cause it's one thing to have been rich
and to have become poor
and it's another just to stay that way.
"What depression?" "Is that your Coca-Cola?"
"Not mine. Never had a nickel to buy one."
Flat and caramel, nary a dust speck on it:
    "In the gloom the gold . . ."
"The Great *what*, Lady Bird?
We already got a Texas."

He lit out and scalped ever' one of them Jacksonians:
"There are no necessary evils."
And so for a hundred and forty years
we had no bank,
and now no one lives
who ever lived without one.

And it's a good thing too
'cause Sherman burnt the fields
and all the paper with 'em,
paper backed by sovereignty,
paper backing sovereignty,
paper which they inflated
faster'n they spent:
"Greater purchasing power
for the government."
"Sounds like witchcraft!" which it was.
And, "Most of Newton's works are on alchemy," which they were.
       Pendragon : Merlin :: Davis : Elmore
that is, Edward C. Elmore, Treasurer, Confederate States of America.
At my mother's house in Alabama

a man came by with a metal detector:
    "Order now and it could be yours for 5 easy payments
        of only $19.99!"
"They started meltin' 'em for bullets.
Turns out they was worse for shootin'
than they was for buyin'!"

He lit out and scalped ever' one of them Jacksonians:
"There are no necessary evils."
And so for a hundred and forty years we had no bank,
just dead Indians.
Representative Samuel "Tripp" Travers, Finance
Committee meeting,
North Carolina State Legislature, whatever July 2012:
"Y'all gonna ha'ta decide: Is you a business,
or is you a go-vern-ment?"
backhanding the round table with each accent.
"Is you a *bus*iness, or is you a *go*-vern-ment?"
knowing the music of his speech.
And then that black-suited Yankee outta Chiraq
got up to the microphone:
"First United National Bank of Illinois
would like to extend low-interest, affordable loans
to the minority community of North Carolina,"
and them that wore Sunday hats nodded,
and them that wore seer-sucker suites guffawed.
And so "Tripp" called him "no better'n a carpet-bagger,"
    which was true,
but Reverend Beardshaver, ever the opportunist,
with his Jheri curls and his oxygen tank
and his *abogado* from the ACLU,
recently returned from defending teenage polygamists in Utah
somewhere between Capitol Reef
and the San Juan goosenecks
where the only radio is about Indians
pickin' shrooms in the park,

called a press conference just to say,
"He's a racist."

And so they moved to Texas,
and it's a good thing too
'cause it's better to have no money
but hogs and heifers and peas and watermelons—
"A hog loves a watermelon," John Reuben would say.
And so he took his state fair prize money,
gave it to his elder brother, Maurice, saying,
"Take and eat."—
than to have money what kills
even worse than it buys.

Race and a Rebel

James B. rented two of Bill Henry's Negroes,
Cicero and Catonis, and rode with the Texas cavalry
down Galveston. And everyone in the regiment
thought him a plantation man because he sublet his Negroes,
you know, to the Wallaces, for to purchase a uniform,
gray wool and gold-trimmed, and a saber.
And when he came back, broke enough to shine light through,
he married his widowed daughter, Kathleen, off to S. R.,
and that's how the devil Joe Abby,
third begotten of two cousins,
conceived in a hailstorm, came to be.

And a whole 20th century passed, and then
(Uncle Claude recounting):
"That drunk ------ ran over my daddy!
He was a-aimin' for him!"
(or he should've been).
"That boy tried all them stunts
he seen in westerns,
standing on the back of the horse,
shootin' pistols over his shoulder.
Gave him nerves like block ice.
Discharged from the Marines
for beatin' a black boy
half to death. Sent to the army
where they needed
more murderous S.O.B.s."

But Uncle Claude never said much more.
He'd rather remember his sweet little Sara
at Pine Hill before the war,
and Joe Abby'd rather remember
little Mrs. Johnnie at sixteen before the war,

and James B.'d rather remember
little Kathleen at the washtub before the war.

At ten years old John Reuben had a great insight:
as he let the ice boy come in through the back door
to deliver the ice, he saw that the boy's overalls
were dirtier and raggedier than his, and he knew
he was not as poor as the black kids
because they had holes in their jeans and he didn't.

And every two years Joe Abby and Joe Bailey
would drive to Dallas, to the hat outlet, and afterwards
sit for a week out in front of the store, all day and all night in vigil,
and be somebody. And Abby would give directions
to all who drove by, though he never owned a car himself.
But the black daddies' hats had holes in their crests,
so they wore no hats on Sundays.

And not too long after emancipation
the freedmen set up the Do Right Church.
Now it just so happened that old Jimmy B.
had himself a son by Mrs. Catonis, and this son
had himself a son by the same namesake
who, being half white on account of his mother
was also half white, learned to read and write
and became an eloquent speaker and school teacher
and the preacher down at the Do Right Church
where on Sunday nights the white folk
would park their cars in the crackling, grasshopper night
and listen to the floor stomping and singing
smoldering from that white place.
Except for Joe Abby, who had no car
on account of he was lazy,
"Lazy as a ------."

ELOISA BRESSAN

A Resurrection

"Mio zio è inventore" sd little Alice
        sitting on Grandpa's couch
"Every family has its own Archimedes."

Archimedes, Pithagoras
There is poetry in numbers
E il κόσμος risuona di dolci melodie . . .
Ma il rumore ci opprime
Ci toglie vita e pensieri
Disturba finanche la sordità
"Inventi il silenzio!"—the prophetess.
"Ci renda lo 'swissscch' delle falci!"

Pithagoras, Archimedes.
"Datemi un punto d'appoggio
       ed io solleverò il mondo."
Γνῶθι σεαυτόν
Papà never knew how to pronounce Greek choruses:
ἄνδρα μοι ἔννεπε Μοῦσα πολύτροπον

You could lift the world,
But that's not enough.
They say it won't do.
Ma l'ispirazione è momentanea.
Gli istanti accadono. Illuminano. Passano.
     ΦΩΣ
Like when I was wandering
In mezzo alle nubi, tra cielo e baratro,
Pensavo fosse il paradiso,
    ma dev'essere il purgatorio.
"You are mistaken," the gentleman said,
"This is no paradise."

But in that couch perspiring poetry
Or under a tree (parapluie improvisé)
"Piove dalle nuvole sparse"
"Sulla favola bella, che ieri t'illuse. . ."
"All ages are contemporaneous!"

Nausicaa glanced at a beautified Odysseus
She lent him a rope
Φαιακοι's island

"You should learn to drink
"To be a poetess."
Boire est un art.
Memories like bricks to build worlds with.

"Had we but world enough?"
We had. J'aurais été une châtelaine magnifique.
"You must be a fairy's child, little Alice."
INFANTES SUPPOSITI
I have the hair of a Saliga.
I brush it every day
Per non rompere il sortilegio.
Poppies in the bedroom, red and yellow,
Poppies, ugly poppies, red and yellow:
Spennellati sulla tela
To soothe my sleep.
Drifting, wandering, losing time.
And love? No sign.
Or else he did, and didn't want me to know.

"You are a memory," he said.
Vivi nella memoria di un'estate sospesa,
The *bruit* of some *fraulein*.
Nothing more than memory.
Pierced like the Virgin in Trento,

Stabbed nella clavicola:
La spada del saggio slashing my verses.

As I entered the ice
And felt the cold, crystal cubes of memory,
Cut with the swischhh of the reaper:
A woman of terror I met
Golden locks of putrefied beauty.
Medusa?
Magic mirror, shield me.
Her glamorous treacherous eyes:
No Perseus there.

"You are stuck in that mirror, little Alice"
A voice from afar
"News of friends from afar"

"You're the fairest in the land," Medusa.
Reaper reaping crops,
I hear you.
Tagliatele la testa!

Years I spent
"Heavy with weeping"

Gusci d'uovo sul focolare,
Food for fairies to come back
And save us SUPPOSITI.

My filters to kill Medusa.

Staring at a dried-up hookah,
sore with nightmares:
"Where is that caterpillar?"
He was supposed to guide me.

Pianto idee in the tower of Shalott
The goddesses' lovers in the names of the flowers.
Le hipster à l'air blasé, Jardins du Luxembourg:
"Flowers, flowers, people, flowers"

And suddenly there
Scintillante voice from The Dream-Land,
Smoky couch of a mushroom
In the garden of the Medicis:
"Good grief"—the poet—"shut up and live!"

MARY DE RACHEWILTZ

THE AAR

My eyes hold many landscapes,
the heart but one, traversed
by the singing river Aar.

Its water springs from glaciers
topping the wide green valley,
my Pusterthal.
              A child's feet
freezing in the wild current
thawed to the knowledge that
wisdom rises through bare feet,
treading water, treading sand,
treading turf in April,
ankle-high fresh grass in May,
prickly stubble in September,
dry leaves in November, while
walking on clods of black earth
behind the plough opening
the furrow for new plantings,
feeling and smelling the snow
squeak under thick leather soles.

To many landscapes I have
added a grassy flavor,
mingling salt water, seaweed
and shells on distant shores,
laying on smooth sunny rocks
or on rolling grey shingle,
I can ever hear the sharp song
              of the Aar.

MEINE AAR

In meinen Augen sind viele Gegenden.
Im Herzen aber nur eine, dort
wo hindurchfliesst die singende Aar.
Ihr Wasser kommt von den Gletschern,
von ganz oben im weiten grünen Land,
meinem Pustertal.

Kinderfüsse haben gefroren
im wilden Fluss.
Sie aber tauten auf, denn weise
wird, wer barfuss geht.
Sie stampften im Wasser,
sie stampften im Sand,
sie stampften auf Humus im April,
im knöchelhohen Gras im Mai,
auf kitzligen Stoppeln im September,
auf trockenem Laub im November,
auf schwarzen Schollen hinter dem Pflug,
der auftat die Furchen für die neue Saat.
Ich spürte und roch den Schnee.
Er gierte unter den dicken Ledersohlen.

Mancher Gegend habe ich
den Geruch von Gras gegeben,
vermischt mit Salzwasser,
mit Algen und Muscheln.
Ich bin an der Sonne gelegen
auf glattem Fels oder losem Geröll.
Doch immer hört ich das Lied meiner Aar.

—*translated by Walter Baumann*

MARY MAXWELL

To Francesco Petrarcha

They've named a motel after you, Petrarch,
        just off the autostrada at Monselice,
                in full view of
                the Euganean Hills.
                There,
        under the seeming endlessness
            of cumulus clouds,
eighteen-wheelers drive
        through fields of sunflowers,
floral sunshine spread beneath a plain of blue uplift.

        Your old haunts have composed themselves
        into a landscape of inverted optimism.

            Though I've never been
the greatest admirer of your poetry,
                I admit that I too have enjoyed
        love's abstraction
considerably more than its actuality, almost
prefer the anticipation of continental travel to
Europe's once nearly unobtainable amenities.

Yet, as a true professional, you'd better accommodate
                its newly internationalized
                and corporate mores
        better than I would,
            given half a chance.

            You traded up:
            Artistic autonomy
for a palace on the Riva degli Schiavoni and
a hillside garden in Arquà in which to retire.

While I,
in the forced good fortune of my independence,
inhabit these seasonally alternating estates
of mind and page,
where I am free to entertain ideas of myself
as one of the poets,
conversing at leisure with immortals.

To Dante Alighieri

On the crowded shores of Lake Garda, Dante,
        they've named a pizzeria
    after your *Commedia*.
Contemporary pilgrims,
      ravenous in body and soul after an afternoon of
      screaming on the roller coasters of Gardaland,
go there for base sustenance.
                            And yet,
      what communion is more divine
than pizza porcini with truffled grana
         and a glass or two of Bardolino?
Giotto's angels or Ravenna's saints
would descend for such sublimity.

For, as you must know, your posterity
reside nearby among the hills of Garganago,
             making poetry
             out of grapes:
Alighieri amarone is especially layered with meaning.

      Some continue to know how to live,
            while others have chosen
the virtual reality tour over an actual visit
     to the renovated Cappella degli Scrovegni.

           But really and truly,
    at the Arena in Verona,
    just as *Aida*'s elephants
    (linked trunk to tail)
    entered in orchestral triumph,
             as on celestial cue
             a full moon rose

up from behind
and then over
the amphitheater's top seats.
And as it tracked
a slow semicircle
across the vaulted sky,
real stars peered out from midnight's drapery.

Your Italy is my Paradise.

To Publius Vergilius Maro

Your august name, Vergil, is attached
                              to a new shopping center
near Mantua, just outside Pietole, where you were born.

This, your natal village, once
                surrounded by ancient farms
                and Etruscan manor homes,
                              is currently graced with
                              an American-style mall.
                For convenience and easy prices,
                locals seem to have grown
                              to love it as much as
my fellow countrymen.

                              If you'd care to accompany
                              me through its hellish halls,
I will play guide to my century's
electronic sights and sounds:
                The cell phone.
                    The bar code.
                              How to swipe a credit card.
Access to an astonishing
array of international goods,
                    some of them really wonderful.

Even I admit the DVD gives the poem a run for its money.

Yet how sweet the quiet of the abandoned piazza
during the long lunch hour when stores are kept closed.
The rock doves' announcement of evening re-openings,
iron keys turning loudly once again in rusty locks.

I want past and present both,
your asperity incorporated into
a laptop's instant gratification—

here, now

gravely chiseled lines such as yours
called forth by my plastic keyboard.

To Valerius Gaius Catullus

Catullus, my most favorite soul, at
    the industrial fringes of Verona
        they've named an airport after you.

How delightful to see you lettered across
    one of its hangars, among lovely wingèd
        things, both natural and mechanical.

      You'd adore air travel, for you'd
          be able to leave a languid lover
             in each capital of the globe
    yet easily return, like
          a swallow, to Sirmione
      and the wines
          of the Colli Veronesi.

   Dio me guardi da chi non beve vino.

Your villa's site on the lake is the most beautiful I've ever seen;
      the locale's thermal baths
         and mountain springs
            taken in alternation
almost compensating for the excesses of urban *dolce vita*.

For what gives more pleasure than
      the tongue and its affiliated arts?
         What is more profound than poetry and love?
As at a plane's unexpected dropping, both
      bestow upon us the distinct sensation that
         heart and mouth are no longer separate.

Momentarily terrifying but worth it, these
paired sailings exist outside of mortal time.

Airblown kisses
    of fond farewell
        or floating feather-down
            loosed from a pillow,
in such heady atmospheres
        our poems also take flight.

* all four poems from *Cultural Tourism* (LongNookBooks) © 2012
Mary Maxwell

BILJANA D. OBRADOVIĆ

FLAG BURNING LESSON

for my VCU MFA classmates 1988–1991

Warren, an American, torched the US flag with his lighter
right in front of the whole group of grad students
on my first 4th of July holiday in America—
because he could as a law had just been passed.

Twenty-five years later I remember how I clicked the camera
taking step-by-step photos til the flag was a little stick
which he threw into the garbage. I wouldn't do it, couldn't,
wasn't allowed to, would never imagine burning my country's flag.

I learned a lesson in dissent that day, but not why do it.
What terrible deed would have to be done
for such hatred to develop in me? But, twenty years later when
the second Gulf War was started, but 9/11 was clearly not the Iraqis'
    fault,

or for Serbs after Bosnia, after Milošević, after Srebrenica or
to burn their own flag and the American after 1999.
I am now one of Warren's people, an American,
but still I don't feel as free as he seemed to be.

Pickled Snakes (Snake Wine)

in memory of Dragoslav Obradović (1932–1999)

We all knew about my father's hatred and fear of snakes.
He wouldn't even look at a picture of one, let alone
look at a live one in a zoo, or one in a nature show on tv.

I, too, was scared of snakes, but not my brother, nor my son.
I could never look at them as a child. Later my husband, not me, took
our son who wanted to look at them at the New Orleans Zoo.

But, the most extreme example of my father's phobia
was when he was going on a Far East diplomatic mail pick up trip, and
a colleague who used to live there asked him to bring back to him

wine with "a pickled snake for virility,"* for increased
        sexual performance.
Due to its high alcohol percentage it's drunk from shot glasses.
Dad found it in China and bought a bottle, but he couldn't sleep
        at night

in his hotel room, aware of the snake's presence in his suitcase.
As soon as he showed it to us when he returned he called the guy up,
asked him to come to pick it up right away. He wouldn't try the drink

after the man offered it to him . . . especially not when he
joked how after he drank the wine he'd chop up the snake and
        eat it too.
All he wanted was for him to take the damned thing away!

* from Salman Rushdie, *Midnight's Children*, p. 119.

RAMSES DEVOTION

*after Ramses the Great (c.1303 BC–1213 BC;
reigned 1279–1213 BC)*

In 1974 Ramses II's redhead mummy was flown to Paris
from Cairo for an examination as it had been

infested with a kind of fungus attacking his body.
Issued an Egyptian passport, that listed

his occupation as "King (deceased),"
the mummy was received at Le Bourget airport,

just outside Paris, with the full military honors
befitting a king. They then killed his fungus.

The examination revealed battle wounds, old fractures,
arthritis and poor circulation, just like the rest of us.

I wondered if when he was alive he had dreamt of flying,
and now actually was, after death over 3000 years

later. Oh, if he only knew what would he have thought?
For a while when I was a teenager I was

obsessed with him, thought his exposed face was
so well preserved. Now, I don't quite

understand my fascination back then.
What did I see in him? But, then again,

this type of trans-world transgression,
or transportation does not occur very often.

Whatever happened to, "May he rest in peace?"
But then, why rest? Fly the friendly skies! Be set free.

THE ANATOMY LESSON

The oldest, permanent anatomical lesson theatre
from 1594 in the Palazzo Bo in Padua, is so tiny,
that you would surely get sick from the smell
of the cadaver, the body parts, the gushing of the blood
for science even though this was done
in the colder months of the year,
as the teacher, perhaps Fallopio (after whom
the Fallopian tube was named) made incisions.

The autopsy practice was illegal.
They'd smuggle bodies at night
through an underground canal
into the room, call the students to observe,
then begin the lesson by candlelight. The windows
were bricked lest someone peeked in
and the table could be turned over to show

an animal instead of a human body.
What could they see even during the daytime—
only lit from above by natural light—not veins?
The students, teachers were surely all male,
but not the corpses perhaps. So, some
young men must have been curious
about female bodies. Still, curing
was only done by releasing blood with leaches,

or by herbs. The dissecting table
was in the middle of the room
surrounded elliptically by five
floors of galleries, amphitheatrical in shape.
They could not see much from the fifth floor,
or could they, surrounded by skeletons
of humans and animals, *Memento Mori?*
All two-hundred Paduan academics were

inside, while the rest, outside barely understood
what the point of it all was. Yet, even though
made of wood, this theatre still stands!
Students observed autopsies often listening
to music, to keep them calm, yet this music
attracted no one outside to give them all away.

The Vermin

In the fall it got cold, and every little creature
wanted a place where it was warm.

When the mouse first appeared she was the one who saw it
first under the desk, and then in the kitchen the second time.

After her son found evidence it had climbed on the kitchen table,
she would never enter the house without turning on the lights.

She dreamt that its small paws climbed on her, while she was asleep.
She dreamt of the mice multiplying, being everywhere.

She bought traps of all kinds: the old-fashioned mechanical ones
set with a piece of cheese, the maze ones with poison inside,

even the sticky type she and her partner had used once before
a long time ago which caught the wiggling critter, still alive.

It had to be removed from the house and let die in the trash.
He had to do it. She would not go near it.

Her friend wanted to lend her a cat, but
the cat was too overweight to care about a mouse.

When the weather became warm again
the mouse went back outside.

Inside she continued to turn all the lights on and leave no food out.
She watched for any signs of the vermin the rest of her life.

RON SMITH

Light Verse

The butterfly thought
      the barn's bottle opener
  a rusty blossom.

    The barn never thinks
about butterfly flutter
      on its weathered side.

    The embossed word's there,
      always there, whether or not
anyone sees it.

    Nary a farmer
at the family reunion.
    When we left, we left.

  But we never left,
      thinks the little boy sleeping
inside this white head.

The moon's a spotlight:
      White wings opening, closing.
    What is it sipping?

The origin of the word haiku is a contracted form of haikai no ku, which means "light verse."

Ever Since

(for Vinnie)

I saw in the *Times*
your chin and forehead and, I guess,
            those small flaps at the corners
    of your future eyes, I've been
                thinking about you,
            not grieving
    exactly, for you or with, just
                thinking, the way you
        might finger a place on your skin
                    that's not really sore,
                but could be
                        and soon.

EXHIBITION

This time through I see
         (after the old lady
    in the first room) that I'm not
            seen, the only eyes
      that meet mine dead
blanks of masks. And *now* I see
        the anuses, so many, so
    lovingly, so puckishly
          placed, puckering.

My cooing friends,
from so far away, see what I saw
      the first time: huge hands
and feet, arms like water arcs, and still
    none of us can find
the guitarist or the guitar. We all clap
      our flimsy hands
   at the acrobat,
      at the coalescing kisses.

The wide-ranging Picasso exhibition in Richmond, Virginia.

Yard Work

The leaves are falling again.
        Somewhere off to the south, crows cry.

      The new knee aches, aches. Infected?
Strong coffee, a favorite pen, comfortable chair.
    The wind muses through the pines,
        oak, sassafras, liver-
colored leaves, fluttering down. Daddy,
    long dead, whispers, *Drove to the last, and unlike*
        my sister and brother took off
      for the boneyard
        before I lost my mind. Momma,
    long dead, nearly sings in her clear, restored voice,
      Free now, no longer trapped
  wordless in a broken body.
          The cat in the smeared window
       looks like our previous two,
    flinches, glares when a leaf flips, scrapes on the slate.
      Look! I might have said last week, *Rabbit!*
(hauling ass from that foam of mums,
        through the open gate)
   if anybody'd been with me.

        Am I the only thing here
          that doesn't want out?

SEAN MARK

In Kinder Times

In kinder times we might have loved
you told me once
to kindle growth or something safe
from old folds, bone-scraps   or a flatted chance
to spell the scene—
                              once we'd passed the shells, mute
and in the light, the train rolled on, cropped shadows and
snarled dogs; and in the smiles
                   that dogged our eyes
under the smart arch, PORTBOU
the sign. And though we loved wasp-like—
            your chin's harp still cast pale day
                         on sheets unblotted by the light—
we'd hoard what little time in paint and brick.
At times you'd say you wanted to return
but it wasn't your country anymore.
Today's cohorts are stern and fit
your mourning fit and simple.

SCHERZO

As consolation for the unlikely event
clutch head to leg in delicate hug—
I'm willing to help the plunge
in statement's groping shape: you know
the laws can still be true, we may show
our trace to those who've lost—
the time on hand, the news it takes.
La lima, he says, *è consumata*
worn down, the file, a blunted
tool we do without; but
if throes of sunny turbulence
conjure death not salty life,
what help can one craft
offer the next?
Hassi a rifar, must be remade,
to try once, to try again—
still *il tempo manca*
and the medium is volatile.

Risorgimento

Face down on the table all I held
in my hand—bent in slight sweat
and snug with vows—portends
a kind of compromise, a shared
sense of where we face;
    one fifty to the day,
blacked by dust we celebrate
the fireworks and swell of being right;
in streets June-young
balloons and claws spawn paltry nuptials.

HANDS

Hands are saintly we might say
in gentle carving or speaking-alive
in clean words and similar folds
of pristine things: fruit pip, milk
thistle, adequate luck.
    But home again,
kingdom and guide,
your hands are freight across the divide.
    Something nice was said
for euphony perhaps,
                    a syllabic
caress that lit the flat with bloodless light:
and the joltless heave was
smart and the cracks precise
    and our foreign hands
      rubbed creases in the mass.

The Unfinished Year

A homophonic translation of Cesare Pavese's "Verrà la morte e avrà i tuoi occhi" (*Verrà la morte e avrà i tuoi occhi*. Turin: Einaudi, 1951)

Over mortal eras, far too low-key
quest more to cheer company
all matter's clear in insomnia
sordid, come vest your remorse
or in vice assure. I too okay
savour now and a vain parole,
a tacit grip, a silent no.
Cosy lie hotel bed made thin
when does the soul yet ply
hell-specked. Oh care spur anxious,
quills adjure sapid ache-noise:
say love vital same nullity.

Per usual too, no mortal regard
over sought eras, far too low-key,
sad recover & remit of vice so
come venerate nestle pick at—
re-emerge advise or more,
come sculpt, tire of labour use,
ascend or mourn sad gurgle mute.

MATTHEW PORTO

BARTOLOMEO CRISTOFORI

Maker of musical instruments

A soundboard of cypress without rosewood
and rounded tone colors of brass
yield a reedier, dry sound, soft and loud,
as the name *piano* half suggests.
And in Padua, you thought the prince was jesting
when he found you on the way back from the carnival—
A Firenze, ho bisogno di un tecnico,
e non solo, ma anche un inventore—
evidently one fascinated by machines,
Fernando: collector of clocks & elaborate instruments.
And your design survived
through the house's decline,
even through a century's simplification and re-invention—
"cypress soundboards and brass strings go together:
sweetness of sound rather than volume or brilliance,"
    (says Chinnery, replica maker, 2010).
And though hard to work in that big room
in the Uffizi, *in questo strepito,*
in your own workshop you produced:
the multi-choired spinettone,
the virginal oval spinet,
keyboards, and a clavicytherium
with an unusual case of ebony
(all at 12 scudi per month).
The piano, a thing of cypress and brass,
of unprecedented exactitude
impressed those of the age,
and so you remain one of a rare breed
of *inventor*: one solely responsible
for a new degree of precision.

The Ruin

From the Anglo-Saxon, ca. ninth or tenth century

A curious wonder is this wild stone—Fate fractured it:
the fixed castle fell here, the giants' work was laid low;
high-reaching roofs were ruined, watchtowers toppled.
The gate is frozen shut and the frost-scored mortar
leaves wide gaps in the storm shelter,
    its strength sapped by age.
Earth's cold embrace holds the proud builders,
long dead in the grip of the ground
while hundreds of generations look on and pass away.
Often the face of this wall, goat-grey,
flushed with crimson lichens,
has stood against storm winds
and watched the rise and fall of kingdoms;
high and wide, it cracked and collapsed.
And the wall-stone still,………………
heaped here…………………………………
…………………savagely scraped……………
grimly ground up,…………………………
……………shining………………………………
ingenious work made by a swift mind;
the renowned craftsman bound up the foundations
with firm metal rings.
            Splendid were these palace halls!
the many bathhouses, the high gables
ringing with a martial clamor, loud and long;
and the mead-halls full of mirth and rapture—
perverted Fate overturned it all:
the dead dropped on all sides,
days of pestilence and famine came,
buried all the swordsmen like plunder;
and their the bulwarks were broken,
the fortifications fell; those who could repair them

were dead and buried—whole hosts of men put to earth.
The failure of this house is apparent:
its red tiles are shed; there's wind-space where was shelter,
and the roof is torn asunder;
steady decay brought down these high walls.
Now the rubble is piled like burial mounds
where of old many men, high of heart and gold-adorned,
wearing war gear and splendid garments
turned wine-flushed faces to their treasure hoard:
silver and precious gems; pearls and jewels
innumerable; a bright city, a broad kingdom.
The stone halls stood, hot streams poured forth;
wide floods of water held in the glistening breast
of the bathhouse; hot in the core, a hospitable place.
They let them flow,...........................
the grey stone covered over..............
...................there the pools were!
When...
It is a kingly thing......................a house
...................a city.........................
....

*Note: This poem survives in fragmentary form.

HINOKI CYPRESS

Globose cones hang in pairs
from *the tree where god stayed*
and its leaves scaly and obtuse
wave stiff, black against
the white sky in Kiso.

Some form the looking-pillar in a Noh;
or a table tennis blade,
or are fashioned into a masu hot with sake.
The scents all the same,
a pungency that can fill a hall.

One remains *where god stayed*:
bearing its teeth, knowing the trim bonsai
and the hay fever and the temples, the shrines,
but all the time its deep red-brown bark
possessed by a god or some such
fierce resisting thing.

JOHN GERY

TRENCH CONFESSION

> *frankness as never before,*
> *disillusions as never told in the old days,*
> *hysterias, trench confessions*
>   —Ezra Pound, *Mauberley*

How do I crawl out of this foxhole?
The bombardment has just stopped
but may resume any moment. My camp
and squadron, best I can tell, no longer
can provide sanctuary. They don't exist.
As I peek over the edge here, where,
before the bombs, we dug for three days
to create this shelter, I know now
I am peeking out from my grave. Only
from innocence could I ever have jumped
willingly into this ditch. Look at the dirt,

mud with all the features of a mother's womb,
save sustenance and warmth: Sticky, soft,
wet, colorless until it clings to my skin,
with its roots that reach to enwrap me
like a mother's arteries, but the only blood
I find belongs to those dead or those dying
all around me. How do I crawl out from here
without the help of a forceps or a long arm
reaching in for me? My whole life I've clung
to the concept of inside as where things matter,
as receptacle and hearth, as source of love.

But now I just want to climb out from here, ex-
tract my lean body, plunged over six feet down,
and escape the condemnation of the suicide,

to get free of "protection" under constant threat.
But when I press my face, soaked and caked
into her muck, against these trench walls, into
the roots that clutch—or I push my fist,
gently, further in, I know then I never can
leave here. And I grieve over my own death
yet grow alert to the keen needs of the earth.
Is *this* the same thing they name *duty*?

CHICKADEE

Not for a second
need I hesitate
on this leaf, aphid
crawling cross it, bait

as appetizing
as seed, since that next
leaf, in wind rising,
offers me its ex-

tra spider, or worm
even—or the top
of the tree where, white,
a larva waits, born
aloft, not to drop
but lift, to alight

on (then in) my beak. I speak
only between sips,
deracinated
by shadows that leak
like sap spent that drips
from trees, nothing fated

not to disappear.
Safe in my pea size,
I can let loose, tear
without compromise

whatever I find,
not for vengeance but
(myself delight blind)
for love, for a nut.

SPARROW IN THE DARK

Early spring, 4 a.m.

Now new buds I can see, even
a place to nest, but this cold snap
has left me in shock. I want
better to sing, not grieve, in
spring this way, would like to flap
and splay my wild wings but can't

so long as I can't find her
on one tree or another
through these dark patches. The wind
bucks my feathers. Behind her
or before her, I'd rather
myself delight than be blind

and shivering—but she won't,
though how well she could, call out,
afraid she will attract notice
other than mine. That limb bent
over there, its twigs about
to burst wide, like a lotus,

could be hers, or only my
imagining of the peace
this night denies me. I freeze
and burn, my drop of blood dry
as clogged ice in water pipes.
The wind tires of my endless gripes.

BLUE JAY

This hunger penetrates my jealousy
like a tick that burrows, with jaw first,
under feathers into me. If I squeeze
between my beak its crackling carcass, we
both break in pain. But mine can't be nursed
slowly, peck by peck, back. No remedies,

short of new flesh, for a parasite,
I've learned. This hunger is desperate,
driven to distraction by her slant
wing drop, as a whole school of ticks bite
hard, cleft into my skin, the part of it
prone to intruders, the part that can't

be plucked, really, nor sucked off by despair,
despite how such sustenance breeds death,
nor dried to a husk, from going this long
this thirsty. She assumes I will not care,
on and on, for her dull, graying breast,
her black, transparent necklace, dampened song,

as she squats on the egg her fat mate,
half attentive, half-nestled from her.
Should I flit elsewhere? Might another tree
feed me as well, or better? How I hate
that her sagging throat has become her
best defense. Shall I ever be free?

From Olga's in Dorsoduro

As wind sea-strong of salt
upon my lips
—Pound, "Fragment to W. C. W.'s Romance"

An Adriatic breeze frees a scent
east of here, drifting in
from the lagoon now—a fish smell
but one you wouldn't mind at table
or lifted from boat docks. I expect

nothing more, unless to delight in it,
nothing more of the long shoulders
of those I love to embrace, nothing
from the *ballate* to the insistent squawks
these seagulls devise, no great reply

nor even an echo of a reply, no new
design laced in thread, despite what I said,
nothing of the kind, nothing blue,
nothing red. I expect only a voice
tacit as sky, cool as good news,

engendering tenderness as soon as
I hear it filter through the light.
Let all evenings subside. Let comfort,
that strangest of all lovers' caresses,
abide, slow to dissolve. Let me render

lines here without request:
nothing not in place, nothing
wise, nothing defrayed
from the rest, nothing more,
nothing less.

Photos of the Event

1.   Schloss Brunnenburg, Dorf Tirol, Italy, home of Mary de Rachewiltz and location of the Ezra Pound International Conference. Photograph by Biljana D. Obradović.

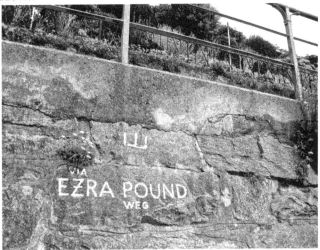

2.   Ezra Pound Weg, Dorf Tirol, Italy. Photograph by Catherine Paul.

3.   Some of the more vocal attendees at the Ezra Pound International Conference. Photograph by Anderson Araujo.

4.   Patrizia de Rachewiltz at Schloss Brunnenburg. Photograph by Biljana D. Obradović.

5.   Church of St. John the Baptist, Dorf Tirol, Italy, near the Bibliothek Tirol, where the reading of *A Packet for Ezra Pound* and the poetry reading took place. Photograph by Catherine Paul.

6.   Readers of *A Packet for Ezra Pound* by W. B. Yeats, Bibliothek Tirol. Left to right: Alec Marsh, Bernard Dew, Peter Liebregts, Roxana Preda, Ron Smith, Justin Kishbaugh, David Cappella, Walter Baumann, Anderson Araujo, Andy Trevathan, Catherine Paul, John Gery. Photograph by Biljana D. Obradović.

7.   Biljana D. Obradović with the poster for the reading event, Schloss Brunnenburg. Photograph by Petar Gery.

8.   Massimo Bacigalupo reading the opening of the "Rapallo" section of *A Packet for Ezra Pound*. Photograph by Biljana D. Obradović.

9.   Audience members at the reading of *A Packet for Ezra Pound*. Photograph by Biljana D. Obradović.

10. Brigitte and Siegfried de Rachewiltz at the reading of *A Packet for Ezra Pound*. Photograph by Biljana D. Obradović.

11. Poets ready to present their work, Bibliothek Tirol. Left to right: David Cappella, Patrizia de Rachewiltz, Catherine Paul, Justin Kishbaugh, David Moody, Stephen Romer, J. R. Forman, Eloisa Bressan, Mary de Rachewiltz, Kenneth Fields, Mary Maxwell, Biljana D. Obradović, Ron Smith, Sean Mark, Matthew Porto, John Gery. Photograph by Svetlana Ehtee.

12. Catherine Paul moderating the poetry reading. Photograph by Svetlana Ehtee.

13. David Cappella reading his poetry. Photograph by Svetlana Ehtee.

14. Justin Kishbaugh reading his poetry. Photograph by Svetlana Ehtee.

15. David Moody reading his poetry. Photograph by Svetlana Ehtee.

16. Stephen Romer reading his poetry. Photograph by Svetlana Ehtee.

17. J. R. Forman reading his poetry. Photograph by Svetlana Ehtee.

18. Eloisa Bressan reading her poetry. Photograph by Svetlana Ehtee.

19. Mary de Rachewiltz reading her poetry. Photograph by Svetlana Ehtee.

20. Walter Baumann reading his translation of a poem by Mary de Rachewiltz. Photograph by Svetlana Ehtee.

21. Mary Maxwell reading her poetry. Photograph by Svetlana Ehtee.

22. Ron Smith reading his poetry. Photograph by Svetlana Ehtee.

23. At the poetry reading, Ron Smith, Sean Mark, Matthew Porto, John Gery. Photograph by Svetlana Ehtee.

CONTRIBUTORS

Walter Baumann was born in Switzerland and studied in Zurich and Aberdeen, Scotland. After two years in Toronto he moved to Northern Ireland, where he taught German and where he is spending his retirement. His hobbies are photography and Ezra Pound, about whom he published two books with the flowery titles *The Rose in the Steel Dust* and *Roses from the Steel Dust*. He has been involved with Pound conferences since 1976.

Born in Italy, transplanted in France, **Eloisa Bressan** has recently moved to the United States, where she is pursuing a doctorate in Comparative Literary Studies at Northwestern University. She holds a B.A. in Classics and a M.A. in Modern Philology from the University of Padua.

David Cappella is a poet and Professor of English at Central Connecticut State University, where he teaches creative writing and literature. He has coauthored two widely used poetry textbooks, *Teaching the Art of Poetry: The Moves* and *A Surge of Language: Teaching Poetry Day to Day*. *Gobbo: A Solitaire's Opera* won the Bright Hill Press Poetry Chapbook Competition in 2006. His novel, *Kindling*, is published by Piscataqua Press. His poems and essays have appeared in various literary journals and anthologies in the United States and Europe. He is currently co-translating *Tracce di un' anima*, a book of poems by the Italian poet Germana Santangelo.

Mary de Rachewiltz grew up in Gais, Pustertal, in Südtirol. She is the daughter of Ezra Pound and the violinist Olga Rudge. In *Discretions* (1971) she tells her life story up to the return in 1958 of her father to Italy. The main fruits of her total dedication to Ezra Pound's heritage are her Italian translations of a selection of Poundian texts, *Opere scelte* (Mondadori 1970) and a complete English / Italian edition of *The Cantos* (Mondadori 1985). Apart from archival work at the Beinecke at Yale, co-organizing exhibitions of Poudiana, and giving lectures on her father's work, she also writes poetry in Italian and English. The poem "Aar" was published in *For the Wrong Reason* (Edgewise Press, 2002).

Patrizia de Rachewiltz grew up in the Tyrolean mountains of northern Italy. She was educated there, in Rome (French Baccalaureat), and in Vienna. She has worked as writer, translator, and language instructor. She lives in 's-Hertogenbosch, the Netherlands. She has published several volumes of poetry: *My Taishan* (Raffaelli Editore, 2007); *Dear Friends*, with photographs by Lynda Smith (Palisade Press, 2008); *Trespassing* (Uno Press, 2008); a volume of prose: *Songs of the Peacock* (Paulist Press, 1977); and numerous translations: *Favole: Fables by e. e. cummings* (All'Insegna del Pesce d'Oro, 1975); *Mr. Wind and Madam Rain* by Paul de Musset (Edizioni C'era una volta, 1994); Pieroing by Soichi Furuta (Greco & Greco, 1996); *The Wind in the Willows* by Kenneth Grahame (Edizioni C'era una volta, 1997); *Eros Psyche* by Michael Lekakis (Raffaelli Editore, 2007); *Your Eyes* by Cesare Pavese (Palisade Press, 2009).

J. R. Forman is the Director of the Writing Lab at the University of Dallas, where he is also a Ph.D. candidate in Literature. A graduate of St. John's College, Santa Fe, he is an alumnus of the University of New Orleans Ezra Pound Center for Literature poetry workshop at Brunnenburg Castle, Italy. He is also the series editor of "Kulchural Affairs" for *Make It New*, the magazine of the Ezra Pound Society. His poetry has appeared in *Ramify*, *White Rock Zine Machine*, and *Ama-Gi Magazine*.

John Gery's seven books of poetry include *The Enemies of Leisure*, *Davenport's Version*, *A Gallery of Ghosts*, and *Have at You Now!* He has also published criticism on a range of modernist and contemporary poets, as well as the book, *Nuclear Annihilation and Contemporary American Poetry: Ways of Nothingness*. With Rosella Mamoli Zorzi and others, he coauthored a walking guide to Ezra Pound's Venice, and with Vahe Baladouni, he wrote a biography of Armenian poet Hmayeak Shems. He has also edited four books of poetry and criticism. Gery has received fellowships from the NEA, the Fulbright Foundation, and the Louisiana Division of the Arts, among others. A Research Professor of English at the University of New Orleans, he directs the Ezra Pound Center for Literature (EPCL), Brunnenburg, Italy. He also serves as Secretary of the Ezra Pound International Conference and is Series Editor for the EPCL Book Series at Clemson University Press.

Justin Kishbaugh earned an M.F.A. in Creative Writing from the Jack Kerouac School of Disembodied Poetics at Naropa University, and a Ph.D. in English Literature from Duquesne University. He published a chapbook of poetry, *For the Blue Flash*, in 2012, and currently serves as the Writing Specialist for Roger Williams University School of Law in Bristol, Rhode Island. Justin's work tends to focus on writing craft, and he places particular emphasis on the interaction between form and content. He is also quite a fan of the Rolling Stones, new shoes, and his cat, Weapon X.

Sean Mark grew up in London and Milan. After a B.A. in Italian from the University of Milan, and an M.A. in English from University College London, he recently completed a Ph.D. in comparative literature at the universities of Tübingen, Bergamo, and Brown, with a fellowship from the European Commission. He has edited and translated two volumes by contemporary Italian poets for Chelsea Editions Press, for which he received the Sonia Raiziss Giop Foundation Grant in Translating. He lives in Paris and teaches at the Sorbonne.

Mary Maxwell is the author of five volumes of poetry: *An Imaginary Hellas, Emporia, Cultural Tourism, Nine Over Sixes,* and the forthcoming *Oral Lake.* Her poetic drama, *Ulysses in Hell,* based on her mother's visits to Ezra Pound at St. Elizabeths, was a finalist for *The Paris Review* Prize. A winner of the 1990 "Discovery" / *The Nation* Award, she has been the recipient of a residential fellowship from the Camargo Foundation in Cassis, France. She has also been a visiting artist at the American Academy in Rome.

David Moody is Professor Emeritus of English and American Literature at the University of York, and author of a three-volume critical biography, *Ezra Pound: Poet.*

Biljana D. Obradović, a Serbian-American poet, translator, critic, Professor of English, and Head of the English Department at Xavier University of Louisiana, has published four collections of poems, most recently *Incognito* (Cincinnati: WordTech Press, 2017); translations of collections of poems into English from Serbian (Bratislav Milanović) and into Serbian from English (John Gery, Stanley Kunitz, Patrizia de Rachewiltz, Bruce Weigl, and Niyi Osundare); and two anthologies of poems, the most recent coedited with Dubravka Djurić, *Cat Painter: An Anthology of Contemporary Serbian Poetry* (New Orleans: Dialogos Press, 2016).

Catherine Paul is Professor Emerita of English at Clemson University. She is author of *Fascist Directive: Ezra Pound and Italian Cultural Nationalism*, and with Margaret Mills Harper, the editor of W. B. Yeats's *A Vision: The Original 1925 Version* and *A Vision: The Revised 1937 Version*. She is now a textile artist at the Greenville Center for Creative Arts.

Matthew Porto is from Long Island, New York. He holds an M.F.A. in poetry from Boston University and a B.A. in English from the University of Scranton. His work has most recently appeared in *SWAMP*, *Strange Horizons*, and *Bird's Thumb*, and is forthcoming in *Crosswinds*.

Stephen Romer is Maître de Conférences at the University of Tours and has lived in France for many years. He writes on different aspects of British and European Modernism and has translated widely from the French, concentrating on modern poetry and fin-de-siècle prose. He has published four full collections of his own poetry and a fifth, *Set Thy Love in Order* is due from Carcanet later in 2017.

Ron Smith, Poet Laureate of Virginia 2014–2016, is the author of three books of poetry from Louisiana State University Press: *The Humility of the Brutes* (2017), *Its Ghostly Workshop* (2013), and *Moon Road* (2007). Smith is also the author of *Running Again in Hollywood Cemetery*, judged "a close runner-up" for the National Poetry Series Open Competition by Margaret Atwood, and subsequently published by University Press of Florida. In 2010 he was named Poetry Editor for *Aethlon: The Journal of Sport Literature*. Smith has been invited to read new poems about Thomas Jefferson and George Washington at Monticello and Mount Vernon, poems about Virginia history and landscape in the Virginia Senate and House of Delegates, as well as poems set in Rome at the Keats-Shelley House and the United States Ambassador's Residence in Rome.